365 Things Every Couple Should Know

HARVEST HOUSE PUBLISHERS
Eugene, Oregon 97402

Published in association with the literary agency of Alive Communications, P.O. Box 49068, Colorado Springs, CO 80949.

365 THINGS EVERY COUPLE SHOULD KNOW

Published by Harvest House Publishers
Eugene, Oregon 97402

Library of Congress Cataloging-in-Publication Data

Fields, Doug
365 things every couple should know / Doug Fields.
p. cm.
ISBN 1-56507-072-0
1. Aphorisms and apothegms. 2. Marriage—Quotations, maxims, etc. 3. Interpersonal relations—Quotations, maxims, etc. I. Title. II. Title: Three hundred sixty-five things every couple should know.
PN6278.M35F54 1993
306.81—dc20 92-33336
CIP

Printed in the United States of America.

96 97 98 99 00 01 \ BF \ 10 9 8 7 6

To Marv & Elva:

Thank you for being a superb example of what 50 years of marriage should be.

Introduction

If you're single or already a couple, *365 Things Every Couple Should Know* is only the beginning of the many ways you can say (to your mate), "I love you" and "I appreciate you."

Making daily deposits into your relational bank account assures you a high rate of return. Most deposits only take an extra moment or two, but the rewards are forever...and they're so easy you'll wonder, "Why didn't I think of that?"

Enjoy!

Doug Fields

Every Couple Should Know . . .

1

to embrace
one another
for no reason.

2

how to affirm your
love by giving your spouse
a homemade surprise.

Every Couple Should Know . . .

3

God's love for your spouse has no conditions.

4

it is easier to complain about a fault than to forgive one.

Every Couple Should Know . . .

5

the qualities
within your spouse
that ignited
your interest
when you first met.

Every Couple Should Know . . .

6

Eve was created
to be a queen.

7

Adam was created
to be a king.

Every Couple Should Know . . .

8

a good surprise
is to have
your spouse's car washed.

9

how to give your spouse
a visible expression of love.

Every Couple Should Know . . .

10

there's no time
like the present to begin
bettering your marriage.

11

how to take
a 30-minute vacation.

12

how to ensure
your criticisms are
constructive
and not destructive.

13

laughter at a spouse's failure
doesn't motivate change.

14

it is fun to be spontaneous:
tickle, dance, or
join your spouse
in the shower.

15

when to abandon
housework for play.

16

not to reprimand
in public
and double the damage.

17

the importance of looking
into your spouse's eyes
while listening.

Every Couple Should Know . . .

18

that God cares
more about your marriage
than you do.

19

when to add
an unanticipated pleasure
to your daily regimen.

Every Couple Should Know . . .

20

your children
will love to hear
your courtship stories.

21

to always
compliment the cook.

22

a failed attempt
at romance
should be countered
with sincere appreciation.

23

God has a different standard
of beauty than we do.

24

the fun shouldn't end
at the wedding.

25

to cherish the
rare moments
of uncontrollable laughter.

26

one compliment a day
isn't too many.

27

how to
"give preference to
one another in honor"
(Romans 12:10).

Every Couple Should Know . . .

28

how to nurture
your spouse's potential.

29

"I love you"
sounds much better than,
"Why didn't you?"

Every Couple Should Know . . .

30

how to bring out the playful child in one another.

31

years will steal beauty from the body but true attraction will delight in aging flesh.

32

empathy is
much more attractive
than apathy.

33

good memories are priceless
no matter what they cost.

34

the importance
of discovering insight
from every problem.

35

your spouse has
positive qualities that
you should affirm regularly.

Every Couple Should Know . . .

36

how to write your spouse a 20-word love note.

37

how to turn *off* the TV and *on* the communication.

38

to not yell
at one another
unless the house is on fire.

39

when to break
the diet restrictions
and pig out.

Every Couple Should Know . . .

40

your spouse's
secret dream.

41

the winner
of the conflict
isn't always the winner.

42

the importance
of courtship
after marriage.

43

please and *thank you*
are not just
for children to say.

Every Couple Should Know . . .

44

how to make
your spouse laugh.

45

positive memories
become anchors
for future storms.

Every Couple Should Know . . .

46

how to evaluate
the vital signs
of your marriage.

47

where to go
when you are free
for 24 hours.

48

one way to show
that you care
is by spending
your spare time
with your spouse.

Every Couple Should Know . . .

49

how to save
for a rainy day.

50

the difference between
what makes your spouse
tick and ticked-off.

Every Couple Should Know . . .

51

how to give your spouse a "second wind."

52

showering together saves water.

53

a day without
"I love you"
is a wasted day.

54

how to cook
your spouse's
favorite meal.

Every Couple Should Know . . .

55

major house projects
may need
to be followed
by minor
marital counseling.

56

the importance
of maintaining
sexual attraction.

57

how to make
a homemade greeting card
for a special occasion.

58

when to
take over responsibilities
and let your spouse
enjoy a bubble bath.

59

how to use
a camera
and photo album
to document
your relationship.

60

a few massage techniques.

61

the fun of buying
a unique gift
your spouse would never buy
for himself or herself.

62

to forget your
wedding-day waist size.

63

a board game, two candles, and a fireplace can help create a romantic home date.

64

your spouse's favorite magazine.

65

the simple intimacy
of holding hands.

66

the importance of having
a "Do Not Disturb" sign.

67

a bird feeder can become
a backyard theater.

68

at least one dining location
that encourages you
to dress up.

69

to celebrate
the little things
in your lives.

70

the importance
of surprise and mystery.

71

the best
sunset-watching location
and frequent it.

72

how to celebrate
your spouse's victories.

Every Couple Should Know . . .

73

to not replace
the evening gown
with a bathrobe.

74

to not replace
a night on the town
with a television show.

75

marriage
creates situations
that should induce
laughter
rather than anger.

76

your spouse's
favorite music.

77

it is important (and fun)
to save love letters.

78

when it is time to do something together to escape immediate pressures.

79

a romantic location within walking distance from your home.

Every Couple Should Know . . .

80

the game of Scrabble
has been known
to ignite
major arguments.

81

their own intimate vocabulary (which is foreign to other family members).

82

the joy of popcorn, photo albums, and old music.

83

it is immature
to run through
the sprinklers . . .
but lots of fun.

84

touch is a powerful form
of communication.

85

it is fun to discover
short love notes
around the house.

86

to be on the lookout
for a creative gift
to express your love.

87

how to travel together without fighting.

88

how to pamper your spouse.

Every Couple Should Know . . .

89

a quality marriage
isn't measured
by how few
problems you have
but by how you
handle the problems.

90

at least one form
of exercise
you can do together.

91

a trip to the local library
isn't as boring
as it might sound.

Every Couple Should Know . . .

92

TV executives
don't care about
marriage communication . . .
divorce means
more TV purchases.

93

a cheerful heart
is good medicine
(Proverbs 17:22).

94

unexpected gifts can
bring great pleasure.

95

a good marriage
is the best gift
you can give your children.

96

marriage should have
more dreams
than nightmares.

97

God has written
a love letter (the Bible)
filled with great principles
for marriage.

98

your spouse wants
to be viewed as attractive.

Every Couple Should Know . . .

99

to take lots of pictures during your vacations.

100

there is no easy answer to marriage problems.

101

Eve probably said,
"God, Adam just
doesn't understand."

102

it's easier to exercise
when it's fun.

103

love and marriage
go together like
a horse and carriage.

104

if sensitivity
had a price tag
it would be expensive.

105

biblical writers refer to the act of sex as "to know."

106

Moses got married and "knew" his wife for a year without working.

Every Couple Should Know . . .

107

A good listener
hears between the lines.

108

to buy your spouse
crazy underwear every year.

109

hints and innuendos
can sometimes be
subtle forms of manipulation.

110

to eat
cookie dough in bed
at least once a year.

Every Couple Should Know . . .

111

verbal intercourse
is more important
than the other type.

112

how to have fun
without money.

113

you should keep your spouse's insecurities private.

114

it is okay to let your spouse take the credit.

Every Couple Should Know . . .

115

the correct answer to
"Do you love me?"
is not,
"I married you, didn't I?"

116

to save your spouse's handmade gifts and cards.

117

the difference between sex and love.

Every Couple Should Know . . .

118

a quick phone call
when you're
going to be late
can diffuse
a potential explosion.

119

marriages are built on small expressions of affection.

120

to not give up . . . miracles do happen.

121

to return kindness
to one another.

122

there are few shortcuts
to genuine intimacy.

Every Couple Should Know . . .

123

how to make
your spouse feel
like a million bucks!

124

divorce wasn't
in God's plan
when He created marriage.

125

how to establish realistic expectations.

126

how to give your spouse a sense of dignity.

Every Couple Should Know . . .

127

to apply
God's definition of love
to your marriage
(see 1 Corinthians 13:4-7).

128

childhood wounds
are not easily healed.

129

when to escape
to an environment
for undivided attention.

Every Couple Should Know . . .

130

comments about physical features that can't be changed are a waste of breath.

Every Couple Should Know . . .

131

how to cherish
and respect one another.

132

how to remain
the "best catch"
for your spouse.

Every Couple Should Know . . .

133

when the
warning light is on,
it's time to stop,
check the engine,
and make adjustments.

134

anger is not
intrinsically evil . . .
resentment is.

135

how to take responsibility
for your actions instead of
blaming your spouse.

136

how to ignite passion.

137

how to face
stressful events
peacefully.

Every Couple Should Know . . .

138

the importance
of being straightforward
about getting
your needs met
and refrain
from manipulation.

Every Couple Should Know . . .

139

to recall constantly
what first attracted you
to your spouse.

140

true forgiveness
goes beyond words
to action.

141

how to stick together when your world falls apart.

142

there are some things about your spouse you simply cannot change.

143

the attractiveness
of a positive attitude.

144

it's okay to read a book
or take a course
on improving your marriage.

145

the value of
hugging your spouse daily.

146

to pray
for one another.

147

anger impairs judgment
and provokes
harmful words.

148

a walk together
is good for both
the heart and the soul.

Every Couple Should Know . . .

149

marriage is more
than a relationship;
it's a skill
that needs to be learned.

150

to speak well of your spouse—in his or her presence *and* absence.

151

physical intimacy is easier to achieve than emotional intimacy.

Every Couple Should Know . . .

152

the nonnegotiables in your marriage.

153

to cut the edge off your tongue.

Every Couple Should Know . . .

154

behaviors that
please your partner.

155

money problems are
a major cause
for divorce.

Every Couple Should Know . . .

156

a man is capable
of becoming more attentive.

157

a woman is capable
of becoming
more sexually responsive.

158

small steps
in the right direction
can produce big results.

159

"do not let the sun
go down on your anger"
(Ephesians 4:26).

Every Couple Should Know . . .

160

to have a
regular date night.

161

ignored problems
will not become solved
on their own.

162

how to express laughter and humor on a daily basis.

163

how to be a good loser.

164

to save
your favorite memories
in a journal.

165

to celebrate Thanksgiving
more than once a year.

166

the importance
of viewing problems
from an alternate viewpoint.

167

never is an ugly word.

Every Couple Should Know . . .

168

specific
problem-solving skills.

169

how to keep
your spouse from becoming
just a roommate.

170

love is a verb.

171

verbs are defined
by their action.

172

to dream big together.

173

how to feel comfortable saying "no" to your spouse's request for sex.

174

how to pinpoint
the real issues
of conflict and avoid
blaming one another.

175

sex doesn't have to
be great every time.

176

the value of creating
a safe environment
to openly
share your feelings.

177

change begins
with one's self.

178

quality dialogue every day has great rewards.

179

how to argue without attacking character.

180

your spouse's opinions are important.

181

the importance of being able to talk comfortably about sex.

Every Couple Should Know . . .

182

how to turn
a negative thought
into a positive statement
before the brain
engages the mouth.

183

a sensuous kiss a day keeps the blood flowing.

184

"Fine" is not the answer for the question, "How are you feeling?"

185

it is better
to help your partner
be on time
instead of
blaming him or her
for being late.

Every Couple Should Know . . .

186

how to communicate feelings during sexual activity.

187

how to interpret your spouse's nonverbal communication.

188

both partners are equally involved in creating the good and bad of a marriage.

189

how to live beneath their means.

Every Couple Should Know . . .

190

an encouraging relationship
begins when you
look for the positives
about your partner.

191

your spouse's
clothing sizes.

192

touch is
a powerful way
to express concern
and appreciation.

193

the silent treatment
was invented
by a kindergartner.

194

the importance of
each other's individuality.

195

how to avoid
the same sexual routine.

196

how to give
a compliment
without adding a qualifier.

Every Couple Should Know . . .

197

it is fun
to switch roles when
it comes to initiation
of sex, dates,
buying groceries, etc.

198

how to complete this sentence to your spouse: "I love you because . . ."

199

when to forgive and how to forget.

Every Couple Should Know . . .

200

how to flirt
with each other.

201

happily married people
do exist.

202

a few simple
ground rules
for resolving conflict.

203

the fun of
a new activity.

204

how to
mutually participate
in decision making.

205

how to appreciate
and accept the differences
in your partner.

Every Couple Should Know . . .

206

to remember
your anniversary
without subtle reminders
from your spouse.

207

sex is not
a four-letter word.

208

patience . . .
and how to exercise it.

209

to find humor
in negative situations.

210

intimacy
can be expressed
without sex and passion.

211

what to do
when your marriage
is no longer
a top priority.

212

to snuggle in front
of a fireplace.

213

the importance
of planning fun
into your schedule.

214

it is okay
to agree to disagree.

215

mature love
is partner-centered.

216

to slow dance
in your underwear . . .
in private.

217

the difference between liking your spouse and loving him or her.

218

to be proud when introducing your mate.

219

how to view life
from your partner's shoes.

220

how to spell
f-l-e-x-i-b-i-l-i-t-y.

221

females tend to perceive emotions better than males.

222

how to comfort the fears of your spouse.

Every Couple Should Know . . .

223

to attack and conquer crises as a team.

224

to not let kids dictate your marriage relationship.

225

sex begins
in the morning
by the way you talk to
and treat one another.

226

it is terrible
to have to
seek approval
from your spouse.

227

women cry five times
more than men.

228

how to move from
competition to cooperation.

229

sticks and stones
are much less painful
than words carelessly spoken.

230

men reach
their sexual peak
at about age 20;
women at about age 35.

231

marriage is a
collision of two worlds.

232

to appreciate
your spouse's occupation.

233

the hurt that is caused
when you fail
to keep your promises.

234

how to make wisdom a marriage partner.

235

to avoid trivial arguments.

236

to express gratefulness for met needs.

237

how to say, "I'm sorry."

238

women's friendships
are typically deeper
than men's.

239

a quality marriage is built
with two people
good at forgiveness.

Every Couple Should Know . . .

240

you must
remove the plank
in your own eye
before pointing
out the speck
in your partner's.

241

encouragement
before marriage
is kindness,
but encouragement
after marriage
is a necessity.

242

to not expect
overnight miracles.

243

how to agree more
and argue less.

244

being the right person
is more important
than trying to
change your spouse
into the right person.

245

marriage is more enjoyable when neither of you cares who wins.

246

how to serve God together.

Every Couple Should Know . . .

247

it is not
the number of years
you are married
that counts
but what you do
during those years.

248

how to make
every anniversary
a special celebration.

249

it is better
to stress *what* is right
instead of *who* is right.

Every Couple Should Know . . .

250

how to openly communicate their sexual desires.

251

to read Song of Solomon together.

252

to save
pleasant thoughts
and good memories
as much as money.

253

to confess
more than to accuse.

254

a few good rules of diplomacy.

255

going the extra mile will burn 400 calories.

256

a soft answer
turns away wrath
(Proverbs 15:1).

257

perfection simply
is not possible.

Every Couple Should Know . . .

258

how to pretend
no one else is alive
when you are being
romantic with your spouse.

Every Couple Should Know . . .

259

to schedule
your mid-life crisis.

260

good communication
is vital to long-term
sexual fulfillment.

261

recognition and praise
from a spouse
is sweeter than
from anyone else.

262

to bathe in optimism.

263

divorce is
to the emotions
what death is to the soul.

264

it is better to be
solution-conscious
rather than problem-oriented.

265

sex is a privilege!

266

how to keep
the wedding bells
from becoming
a distant sound.

Every Couple Should Know . . .

267

the importance
of a weekly meeting
to discuss problems,
family, calendar, goals,
finances, and so on.

268

a growing marriage
gets stronger and better
over the years.

269

to listen
more than talk.

270

how to be
your spouse's
head cheerleader.

271

romance isn't tied
to just anniversaries
and Valentine's Day.

272

the past is past . . .
move on.

273

a healthy marriage
precedes
a healthy family.

Every Couple Should Know . . .

274

the pleasure
of recalling
the fun you had
before you were married.

275

to not use humor
at your spouse's expense.

276

some nearby scenic spots
you can visit to
appreciate God's creation.

277

the strongest marriages move beyond lovers to best friends.

278

how to spoil your spouse.

279

to share
in financial decisions . . .
the wisdom of two
is greater than one.

280

voice tone
says it all.

281

the strength
of gentleness.

282

it takes only
a second to smile,
but the impression you make
can last for hours.

Every Couple Should Know . . .

283

an exemplary marriage
is the best type
of preaching
your children will ever
hear and see.

284

orgasm isn't the name of a biblical city.

285

to kiss when stuck in traffic.

Every Couple Should Know . . .

286

Ephesians 5:22,28
in a nutshell:
Husbands, love your
wife as yourself
and wives,
respect your husband.

Every Couple Should Know . . .

287

to greet your spouse with an affectionate welcome when he or she comes home.

288

when your spouse needs to hear she is beautiful or he is handsome.

289

God created sexual desire.

290

reliving past disputes
is a sign of
nonforgiveness.

291

a broken heart
leaves room
for God to enter.

292

they need
a weekend retreat
at least twice a year.

293

how to keep
from misinterpreting
your spouse's feelings.

294

how to cure
your partner's headaches.

295

honesty can hurt
but lying will scar.

296

marriage is
a team sport.

297

Cinderella and
Prince Charming
are fairy-tale characters.

298

marriage is permanent
but parenting
is temporary.

299

Hollywood romances
are not filmed
in the world of reality.

300

to pray for
strength and sensitivity.

301

to stop and
celebrate sunsets.

302

there is nothing permanent
about a spouse . . .
except change.

303

the incredible feeling
of true companionship.

304

how to express affection without sexual expectation.

305

your spouse's potential.

Every Couple Should Know . . .

306

you don't need
to be embarrassed
about receiving
professional help
for a marital tune-up.

307

a healthy marriage
can make you something,
while a poor marriage
can reduce you to nothing.

308

failure is a situation and not a person.

309

when to constructively criticize and when to remain silent.

Every Couple Should Know . . .

310

Scripture's encouragement for you to love your spouse as Christ loved His church.

311

how to put together
a first-class evening
for a first-class spouse.

312

marriages rarely blow out . . .
they usually end
through slow leaks.

313

how to
sexually surprise
your spouse.

314

the best exercise
for the heart
is building up one another.

315

how to make
the Christmas season
unforgettable.

316

to keep intimate secrets
just that—secret.

317

to not point out a fault unless you are willing to help your spouse overcome it.

318

when to back off.

319

pride rests
at the root of
most marital conflicts.

320

a good marriage is
the most rewarding form
of human intimacy.

321

"Why are you so upset?" is usually a dumb and obvious question.

322

that God can meet every single one of your needs.

Every Couple Should Know . . .

323

the largest and healthiest sex organ is the brain.

324

the value of a slow reaction.

Every Couple Should Know . . .

325

your spouse's fear
can turn into courage
with the right amount
of encouragement.

326

the joy of making up after a lover's quarrel.

327

sexual satisfaction was part of God's design for marriage.

328

lasting relationships don't just happen.

329

television has a lethal gas known to kill romance.

Every Couple Should Know . . .

330

there are many
rich divorced couples
who would gladly exchange
their money
for their marriage.

331

to ask for
your spouse's advice.

332

great sex won't help
emotional problems
disappear.

333

if your like
for your spouse fades,
the love will
soon die also.

334

it's much easier to find
weaknesses than strengths.

335

guidelines for a great marriage won't work unless you apply them.

336

the importance of appreciating the little things your spouse does.

337

it's better to ask
than to assume.

338

it is more important
to understand
your spouse's feelings
than to explain them.

339

your spouse's needs ought to come before your personal activities.

340

how to express anger without constantly saying the word *you*.

341

a man's sex drive
is similar to
a drum solo.

342

a woman's sex drive
is similar to
a finely tuned orchestra.

343

a few ways to catch your spouse's interest.

344

liking your spouse is as important as loving him or her.

345

a man's knowledge
of his wife's real needs
is primitive.

346

to work on
a few projects together.

Every Couple Should Know . . .

347

to refuse finding sexual satisfaction with others.

348

to shatter the *superior* versus *inferior* roles.

349

forgiveness is
a lifelong process.

350

criticism isn't
an effective form
of foreplay.

351

genuine love is
valuing a spouse
as God does.

352

how to help each other
eat without spilling
while driving in the car.

Every Couple Should Know . . .

353

no matter how busy
your spouse is,
he or she will always
have time for
a favorite hobby.

354

sexual desire
is not necessarily love.

355

these four
dangerous words:
I told you so.

356

how to create
a sense of curiosity
before sharing
important information.

357

the triggers
that hurt feelings.

358

how to comfort with gentleness and silence.

359

the value of a hug.

360

simple is
usually better.

361

the beautiful butterfly
was once a caterpillar.

362

gratefulness expressed through encouragement is a strong motivator.

363

to move your primary focus from your spouse to God.

Every Couple Should Know . . .

364

the more valuable
the possession,
the better
you care for it.

365

your spouse
is priceless.

About the Author

Doug Fields, founder and director of *Making Young Lives Count*, is a national public speaker, college professor, and author of over 12 books including *Creative Romance* and *Too Old, Too Soon*. He serves as director of youth ministry at Saddleback Valley Community Church in Mission Viejo, California.

For further information regarding *Making Young Lives Count* or a brochure of more resources, please call or write Doug Fields at:

Making Young Lives Count
21612 Plano Trabuco Rd.
Suite Q-30
Trabuco Canyon, CA 92679
(714) 459-9517